WHALES SET II

MINKE WHALES

Kristin Petrie
ABDO Publishing Company

visit us at
www.abdopub.com

Published by ABDO Publishing Company, 4940 Viking Drive, Edina, Minnesota 55435.
Copyright © 2006 by Abdo Consulting Group, Inc. International copyrights reserved in all
countries. No part of this book may be reproduced in any form without written permission from
the publisher. The Checkerboard Library™ is a trademark and logo of ABDO Publishing
Company.

Printed in the United States.

Cover Photo: © Lin Sutherland / SeaPics.com
Interior Photos: Brandon Cole p. 21; Corbis pp. 8, 13; © Doug Perrine/HWRF/NMFS permit
    #633/ SeaPics.com p. 17; © Kike Calvo /V&W/ SeaPics.com pp. 5, 19; © Lin Sutherland /
    SeaPics.com p. 11; © Lori Mazzuca / SeaPics.com p. 12; © Robin W. Baird / SeaPics.com
    p. 15; Uko Gorter pp. 6-7

Series Coordinator: Stephanie Hedlund
Editors: Stephanie Hedlund, Megan Murphy
Art Direction & Maps: Neil Klinepier

Library of Congress Cataloging-in-Publication Data

Petrie, Kristin, 1970-
    Minke whales / Kristin Petrie.
        p. cm. -- (Whales. Set II)
    Includes bibliographical references.
    ISBN 1-59679-310-4
    1. Minke whale--Juvenile literature. I. Title.

QL737.C424P39 2006
599.5'24--dc22

                                                                    2005045292

CONTENTS

Minke Whales and Family

In the animal kingdom, there is a group of mammals called **Cetacea**. These animals include the toothed whales, or Odontoceti. The **baleen** whales, called Mysticeti, are also in the Cetacea group.

Baleen whales are filter feeders. This means they obtain food by swimming with their mouths open. One baleen whale family is called Balaenopteridae. Members of this family are **rorqual** whales. Their throat grooves allow huge amounts of water to pass by each baleen plate.

Balaenoptera acutorostrata, or minke whales, are the smallest of the rorqual whales. But, they are the most common baleen whale. Minke whales are small, speedy, and nosy! They are known to approach boats, take a peek, and then disappear.

Huron County Library

Library name: Exeter Branch Library
User ID: 06492001668683

Title: Minke whales
Date due: October 20, 2010 11:59 PM

Title: Fin whales
Date due: October 20, 2010 11:59 PM

Title: Pilot whales
Date due: October 20, 2010 11:59 PM

Visit us at
www.huroncounty.ca/library

Minke whales like to inspect boats. Some species will also swim with divers!

SHAPE, SIZE, AND COLOR

Even though they are the smallest **rorqual** whale, minke whales are big! They grow to be about 35 feet (10 m) long and weigh about 10 tons (9 t). Females are slightly bigger than males.

A Minke Whale

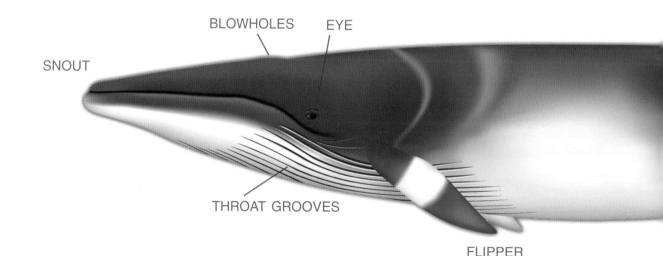

SNOUT

BLOWHOLES   EYE

THROAT GROOVES

FLIPPER

The minke whale's large size gives it a stocky but sleek appearance. These whales have a V-shaped head, a sharp snout, and 50 to 70 throat grooves. These grooves reach all the way past their flippers.

Minke whales have long, pointed flippers and a rounded belly. On their back is a tall **dorsal** fin. Low ridges lead to two broad, pointed flukes. These flukes make up the wide tail fin.

Minke whales are dark gray on their backs and sides. They have a lighter gray or white belly. All minke whales have a distinctive white band on each flipper. Some whales also have V-shaped stripes behind their flippers.

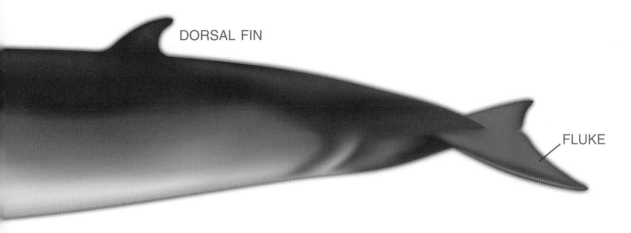

DORSAL FIN

FLUKE

WHERE THEY LIVE

Minke whales are found in most oceans. However, they are divided into several groups. These divisions are based on where the whales are found. There are the North Atlantic Ocean, North Pacific Ocean, and Southern **Hemisphere** groups.

The Antarctic minke is a separate minke species that is found in the Southern Ocean.

All of the groups like cold water. Minkes live closer to the poles than any other **rorqual** whale. They have even been known to get frozen into the ice! Surprisingly, this mammal is also found in mild to warm regions. For this reason, minkes enjoy a very large home!

Minke whales mainly stay out in the open ocean. However, they are known to come close to shore. They may even venture into bays and **estuaries**.

Minke whales also **migrate**. They change their
homes with the seasons and water temperature. They
also migrate to follow their food supply. However, some
minke whales never migrate at all.

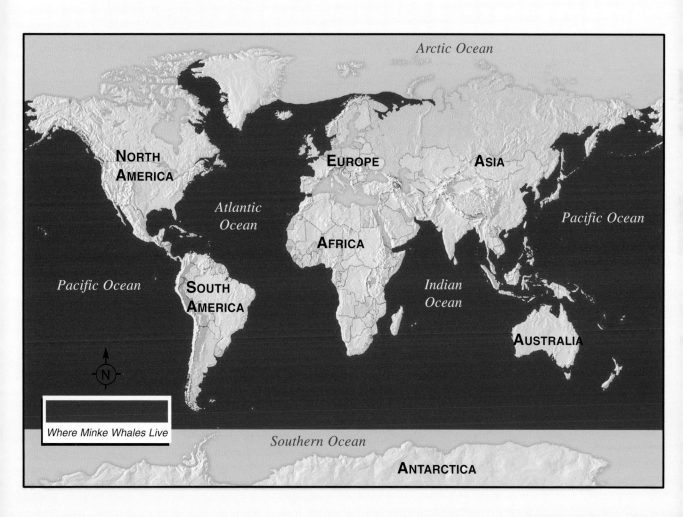

Where Minke Whales Live

SENSES

With such a large **habitat**, it can be difficult for a minke whale to find its way around. Like all whales, its eyes have adapted to seeing underwater. But, it can only see so far. So, a minke whale uses another sense.

Hearing is the most important sense for all **cetaceans**. Whales have ears that humans cannot see. These ears are surrounded by **blubber**. But, minke whales can tell the difference between many calls and songs.

Minke whales are loud. They make noises as loud as an airplane taking off! These noises may be in the form of grunts, thuds, or rasps. They help minke whales find their friends and other whales.

Minke whales are **baleen** whales, so they do not use echolocation. This is a process some mammals use to turn the noise they make into information.

Unlike minke whales, toothed whales use echolocation. First, they send a noise through the water. Next, the noise bounces off another object and returns. The whale learns things from this echoed noise. Echolocation can help a whale determine its location, avoid danger, or find food.

Baleen whales may have some sense of smell. They use this sense to find food instead of using echolocation.

DEFENSE

Minke whales have just two **predators**. One is the killer whale. However, a larger threat is humans. The minke whale's best defense is its speed. These whales avoid predators by quickly swimming away. Their faint **blows** also make them hard for whalers to spot.

When hunting, a killer whale will keep its victim at the surface. It won't let its prey dive and escape.

For many years, these small whales roamed freely. Whalers hunted larger whales because they provided more meat, **blubber**, and other products. But, humans started hunting the minke whale when the larger whales grew scarce.

Between 1970 and 1986, minkes were harvested in great numbers. Whalers were then asked to decrease their take of minke whales. This helped keep minkes from becoming **endangered**.

Whalers towing their minke catch

Today, minke whales are the most common **baleen** whale. It is estimated that there are 800,000 of these whales alive today! Unfortunately, some countries have resumed hunting the minke whale.

Food

Baleen whales have large mouths. So, you would think they eat big animals. However, baleen whales do just the opposite. They feast on the ocean's smallest creatures.

The minke whale's favorite foods include **plankton** and krill. They also enjoy sardines, anchovies, cod, and herring. Minke whales get this food in several ways, including gulp feeding and skim feeding.

To gulp feed, a minke whale rushes through the water with its mouth open. To skim feed, it simply swims with an open mouth. The minke's many throat grooves allow its mouth to get really wide with either method. Tons of water enters and passes by its baleen plates.

Baleen plates are adapted to catch all kinds of prey. The outer side of each plate is smooth. But, the inside

Baleen whales also lunge feed. This is when a whale rushes to the surface of the water with its mouth open to catch food.

is frayed to act as a strainer. When the whale closes its mouth, all the water is pushed out. The prey, on the other hand, heads to the whale's stomach.

BABIES

The minke whale is ready to reproduce at six years of age. Mating takes place in winter when the minke whale has **migrated** to warmer waters. Mating rituals are not well-known. However, mating appears to take place in shallow waters.

A female minke whale is **pregnant** for about ten months. She returns to shallow, warm water to give birth. Baby minke whales are called calves. Minke calves are 9 feet (3 m) long and about 700 pounds (320 kg) at birth!

A mother whale helps her new calf to the surface immediately after birth. After its first breath, the calf begins to swim. A female minke nurses her young with milk for six months. They stick together for about one year. Minke whales have a life span of about 50 years.

Humpbacks and other whales help their calves to the surface, too.

BEHAVIORS

Minke whales are often found alone. But small groups, or pods, of two to three whales gather for certain reasons. For example, two to three whales may stick together for **migrating** and feeding. Also, a mother and calf will stay together for about one year.

These solitary animals swim near the ocean's surface. Their dives usually last between 10 and 15 minutes. Longer dives last up to 25 minutes. At the end of a dive, they exhale before surfacing. This makes their **blow** less noticeable than other whales.

Minke whales are curious. They like to approach boats. After a quick peek, they will arch their back and dive. On other occasions, minke whales swim alongside ships. They can keep up with vessels traveling about 16 to 21 miles per hour (26 to 34 km/h)!

Minke whales release air from their two blowholes before they reach the surface. This makes their blow less noticeable even though it rises seven feet (2 m) above the water!

MINKE WHALE FACTS

Scientific Name: *Balaenoptera acutorostrata*

Common Name: Minke Whale

Other Names: Little Piked Whale, Pike Whale, Little Finner, Lesser Finback, Pikehead, Sharpheaded Finner, Lesser Rorqual

Average Size:
Length - 35 feet (10 m)
Weight - 10 tons (9 t)

Where They Are Found: Most oceans of the world

*The dwarf minke whale
is a subspecies of the
minke whale. So, it is
not its own species. It is
the Southern Hemisphere
group of minke whales.*

GLOSSARY

baleen - of or relating to the tough, hornlike material that hangs from the upper jaw of certain whales. Baleen is used to filter food.

blow - a mix of air and water droplets that are released when a marine mammal breathes.

blubber - a layer of fat in whales and other marine mammals. Blubber provides the whale with insulation, food storage, and padding.

Cetacea - an order of mammal, such as the whale, that lives in the water like fish. Members of this order are called cetaceans.

dorsal - located near or on the back, especially of an animal.

endangered - in danger of becoming extinct.

estuary - the body of water where a river's current meets an ocean's tide.

habitat - a place where a living thing is naturally found.

hemisphere - one half of Earth.

migrate - to move from one place to another, often to find food.

plankton - small animals and plants that float in a body of water.

predator - an animal that kills and eats other animals.

pregnant - having one or more babies growing within the body.

rorqual - any baleen whale with grooves that allow its throat to expand for feeding.

WEB SITES

To learn more about minke whales, visit ABDO Publishing Company on the World Wide Web at **www.abdopub.com**. Web sites about these whales are featured on our Book Links page. These links are routinely monitored and updated to provide the most current information available.

INDEX